BRITISH
STEAM LOCOMOTIVES

A Colourmaster Publication

As the wide-spread commercial use of steam locomotives recedes further and further into the past, public interest in the old steam age seems to grow. The number and popularity of railway museums and exhibitions is on the increase, the enterprising little narrow gauge steam railways are attracting more holiday passengers than they did, while steam railway enthusiasts of all ages are constantly on the watch for new or for revised colour illustrated publications. This is an inexpensive but high quality distillation of two Blandford Press publications in their Pocket Encyclopedia series entitled British Steam Locomotives in Colour and Steam Railways of Britain in Colour and we are grateful to them for allowing us to use selections from their art work and from Mr O. S. Nock's authoritative text.

LIVERPOOL AND MANCHESTER RAILWAY. 1829

The 'Rocket' built by Robert Stephenson and winner of the Rainhill trials.

While very far from being the father of all steam locomotives the *Rocket*, winner of the ever-famous Rainhill trials of 1829, could certainly lay claim to be the very first one to be reasonably successful and reliable in service. In the Science Museum at South Kensington there are, virtually, two *Rockets*. One, an old and obviously well-used machine, is the original engine, though very much altered from the condition in which she won the Rainhill prize for George and Robert Stephenson. The second is an exact replica of the original, in her Rainhill condition, in the gay livery she sported for the trials. The *Rocket* as originally built, and as illustrated here, had her cylinders mounted at a steeply inclined angle high up on the side of the boiler. This gave her an awkward swaying action at speed, and some little time after she went into regular service on the Liverpool and Manchester Railway the position of the cylinders was changed. The other outstanding feature of the original *Rocket* was the use of the multitubular boiler, and the passing of the exhaust steam from the cylinders through a narrowing passage to an orifice in the smokebox. The blastpipe, for so it became known, produced a draught through the boiler tubes and assisted in accelerating combusion of the fuel, and the rapid raising of steam.

NORTH LONDON RAILWAY. 1868

An Adams 4-4-0 tank, as modernised and running in the 20th Century.

William Adams was one of the many locomotive engineers of Victorian times who moved rapidly from one railway to another. Examples of his fine work were eventually to be found not only on the North London, but also on the Great Eastern, on the London, Tilbury and Southend, and most distinguished of all, on the London and South Western. Generally he favoured outside cylinders and his 4-4-0 tank design for the North London was originally turned out in the same brilliant and ornate style as the inside cylinder 4-4-0. This style of painting was continued on the North London Railway until 1882, after which a livery corresponding closely to that of the London and North Western Railway was adopted. It is in this form that the Adams 4-4-0 tank is illustrated. It was in such form that these powerful and efficient little engines became familiar to thousands of season-ticket holders travelling to and from the City terminus at Broad Street. They worked trains of little four-wheeled coaches, seemingly of caravan length, over the Great Northern main line to Potters Bar, and to High Barnet over a steeply graded branch. They were familiar on this duty well into the nineteen-twenties. On these trains they carried the destination on a huge board that extended almost to the full width of the buffer beam.

FESTINIOG RAILWAY. 1869
Robert Fairlie's patent 'double engine' as running today.

The Festiniog Railway was built to convey slates from the quarries of Blaenau Festiniog to Portmadoc for shipment, and while heavy loaded trains could be worked down the valley without difficulty there was congestion on the line because of the limited loads of empties that could be hauled up the steep gradients from the coast. Robert Fairlie then devised the famous double-engine, consisting of two engine units, back to back, with two boilers fed from a central double firebox. Although the double boiler is built as a single unit structurally, there are actually separate fireboxes and separate firedoors. The water and steam space is continuous throughout. The first 'double engine', the *Little Wonder* showed its ability to haul more than twice the load of any engine already on the line, and after 1869 a number of double engines were put to work. Two of them still survive today, and after lying derelict in the Boston Lodge Works for very many years both have been restored to first-class working order, and are giving excellent service on the railway today. The Fairlie articulated engines of the Festiniog Railway represent a most historic development in steam locomotives. The principle of articulation, so putting what is virtually an assembly of two engines under the control of a single crew, was developed strikingly in the Beyer-Garratt type of locomotive, to which reference is made later.

LONDON, CHATHAM AND DOVER RAILWAY. 1873

One of Martley's 'Europa' Class 2-4-0s used on the Dover Mails.

In 1873 the Chatham Railway gained the exclusive contract for carrying the Royal Mail between London and Dover, and to ensure punctuality the Locomotive Superintendent, William Martley, was instructed to provide four new locomotives of enhanced power. Few engines of a small class have, in relation to their small numbers, gained praise or fame to a greater extent than these splendid little 2-4-0s, which were named *Europa, Asia, Africa* and *America*. They immediately became known as the 'Mail Engines', and became familiar and popular with the travelling public from their handsome appearance and excellent work. These trains stopped at Herne Hill, to attach or detach the City portions, and the 74 'les between Herne Hill and Dover town were booked to be covered at an average speed of about 47 m.p.h. At the height of the Chatham Company's Continental mail traffic there were seven expresses daily booked to make an overall average

speed of 44 m.p.h. between Victoria and Dover Pier. In 1873-8, the hey-day of the 'Europa' class, this was excellent going over a hilly road. They were fitted with new boilers in 1892 and survived to carry the gay S.E.&C.R. livery. In the present century they continued to be called upon for express work, and they were not finally withdrawn from traffic until 1907-8.

CAMBRIAN RAILWAYS. 1893

A passenger 4-4-0 designed by Aston.

The Cambrian Railways – always in the plural – was a difficult system to manage, with its main line running from Whitchurch up the Severn Valley, and then through mountainous country to the sea at Aberystwyth, and some very long and meandering branches. Furthermore, its administrative headquarters and locomotive works was clean outside Wales, at Oswestry, in Shropshire. From Dovey Junction a line made its way right round the northern arc of Cardigan Bay to Pwllheli, while from Moat Lane Junction another line followed a chain of valleys in Central Wales, to Brecon. And yet, for all its far flung extent the Cambrian had much more of a main line character than the busy local railways of South Wales. Its trains savoured of long-time, if not long-distance travel, and this was reflected in the locomotive power employed. Very few tank engines were used, and on the main line trains a change was made from the 2-4-0 to the 4-4-0 type of tender

engine in 1878. The engine shown in our picture is of a later and much larger class, designed by Mr Aston and first built by Sharp, Stewart and Company in 1893. They were excellent machines, and for many years hauled the main line trains, carrying through carriages from Aberystwyth to Manchester, Birmingham and London. The Cambrian engines, although painted black, had the distinction of carrying the insignia of the Prince of Wales on their tenders.

THE HIGHLAND RAILWAY. 1896

A David Jones 4-4-0 'Loch', used on the Perth-Inverness run.

In his earlier 4-4-0 locomotives for the Highland Railway Jones had perpetuated the massive double framing at the front end, with the outside cylinders snugly ensconced between the two parts of the framing, and very rigidly secured thereby. This was a legacy from the practice of Alexander Allan, when locomotive construction had scarcely emerged from its infancy and there was difficulty sometimes in maintaining the cylinder fastening secure. In 1896, when the majority of British engines still favoured inside cylinders, Jones retained them outside, but with greatly improved constructional methods abandoned the double framing on the 'Lochs', and produced an extremely simple locomotive thereby. The 'Lochs' were in the very top flight among passenger engines of the day. Massively built, skilfully designed, and economical to run, they quickly became great favourites with their drivers. This, Jones's successor in office

learned some years later. On a very special occasion the new engineer intended to run an express from Perth to Inverness with two of his own engines. The men demanded that on such an auspicious occasion they must have two Jones 4-4-0s; the newer ones were not *suitable!* Many years later, during World War I, when additional engines were needed for the wartime traffic, three more 'Lochs' were built to the original drawings of 1896. A fine tribute to an excellent design.

GREAT NORTH OF SCOTLAND RAILWAY. 1920
A particularly handsome 4-4-0 by T. E. Heywood

Following the resignation of W. Cowan, the G.N.S.R. was served successively by two engineers who later moved to much larger Scottish Railways: James Manson, who went to the Glasgow and South Western, and W. Pickersgill, who went to the Caledonian. In 1899 Pickersgill designed a particularly handsome 4-4-0, and ten were ordered from Neilson and Co. of Glasgow. When the time came for delivery, traffic on the G.N.S.R. had declined to such an extent that the Company could not afford them, and five were purchased by the English South Eastern and Chatham Railway. But the five taken by the G.N.S.R. became the first of the final development of motive power on the railway, and eight further engines of the class were built at Inverurie Works between 1909 and 1915. After World War I when T. E. Heywood had succeeded Pickersgill as Locomotive Superintendent, eight new 4-4-0s were added to the stock, similar to Pickersgill's

1899 class, but having superheaters. The eight engines of the new superheater class were all named, and it is one of these, the *Gordon Highlander*, that has been preserved. In Heywood's time the picturesque green livery of the locomotives was superseded by black, and in G.N.S.R. days the *Gordon Highlander* never carried the original green. When the engine was withdrawn for preservation and restored, it was painted in the green livery, as shown in our picture.

LANCASHIRE AND YORKSHIRE RAILWAY. 1899
An Aspinall 'Atlantic' 4-4-2

It was a race between the Great Northern and the Lancashire and Yorkshire Railway as to which would produce the first Atlantic engine to run in Great Britain. The Great Northern won the race, but the Lancashire produced an engine of great character and distinction. In some ways the 'Highflyers', so called because of the high pitch of their boilers, could be described as an enlarged and elongated version of Aspinall's 4-4-0 of 1891. But the 'Atlantics' were notable in having a very large boiler, and a Belpaire firebox, both of which features placed them far apart from the 4-4-os. They were designed for high speed running over all parts of the system with heavier trains than could be taken by the 4-4-os. When they first appeared in 1899, locomotive enthusiasts and railwaymen alike were positively staggered by the size of these 'Atlantics', and their running, particularly on the Liverpool and Manchester service, was at times breathtaking, not only in the maximum speeds attained but in their acceleration from rest. With them it was nothing to pass Salford, a mere $\frac{3}{4}$ mile out of Manchester, at over 50 m.p.h. On a trial run from Liverpool to Southport, in 1899, with a 5-coach train, one of them is reported to have attained a speed of almost 100 m.p.h. All 40 of them passed into L.M.S.R. ownership, and the last of them was not scrapped until October 1933.

GREAT EASTERN RAILWAY. 1900

The 'Claud Hamilton', a 4-4-0 express passenger locomotive.

For upwards of 40 years successive locomotive superintendents of the Great Eastern Railway had built little save single-driver express locomotives. Where there had been coupled engines, as with the otherwise identical '1000' class 2-2-2, and 'T.19' 2-4-0 of James Holden, the singles had proved as good as, if not better than, the coupled engines. But by the turn of the century something considerably larger was needed. The crack expresses were being equipped with corridor coaches throughout, and restaurant cars, and the loads of the holiday trains were rising from 250 to 350 tons. Under James Holden's supervision the *Claud Hamilton* engine was designed and built at Stratford, in 1900. It was much larger and more powerful than anything previously seen on the G.E.R., and where the 'singles' had tackled trains up to 250 tons in weight, the 'Claud Hamilton' class 4-4-0s could, when really extended, take *four hundred* tons. Again, while most of

the 'singles' had a very short life some of the 'Claud Hamiltons', through various processes of rebuilding, lasted for more than fifty years. The first engine, No. 1900, was the only one to be named, after Lord Claud Hamilton, the Chairman of the Great Eastern Railway. The original design had a boiler with a round-topped firebox, but later varieties were fitted with Belpaire types. They rank among the most successful 4-4-0 express passenger locomotives ever built.

GREAT WESTERN RAILWAY. 1903
The 'City of Truro', a record breaking design.

These locomotives, although relatively few in number, gained great fame for their designer, for the G.W.R., and for British railways. Technically they represent an important link in the chain of development of locomotive practice at Swindon, from the Victorian traditions of the Dean period to twentieth-century standards. They retained the outside frames of former days, and cylinders with slide valves, but incorporated the very important advance of the tapered-barrel boiler, and Belpaire firebox. In high-speed express traffic with trains of moderate weight they were outstandingly successful, improving upon the new standards of running set by immediate predecessors of the 'Atbara' class, which were similar, but with parallel boilers. Engine No. 3433 *City of Bath* set up a new record for the London–Plymouth run made non-stop, via Bristol, in 233½ min. for the distance of 246·6 miles; this record was made with an advance

portion of the Cornishman express in 1903. Engine No. 3440 *City of Truro* reached a maximum speed of slightly over 100 m.p.h. near Wellington, with an Ocean Mail special in May 1904. In ordinary service these engines were responsible for the first regular running of the Cornish Riviera Express non-stop in each direction between Paddington and Plymouth 245·6 miles in 267 min. The *City of Truro* is now in the Great Western Railway Museum at Swindon.

GLASGOW AND SOUTH WESTERN RAILWAY. 1903
A Manson 4-6-0 for the Midland 'Pullman' trains.

The Anglo-Scottish expresses following the Midland route from St Pancras to Carlisle were sharply timed, and greater engine power was needed than that afforded by the Manson 4-4-0s of 1892. The 4-6-0s built in 1903 were in every way a typical Manson design, in their neatness of outline and simplicity of detail. The drivers took to them at once, because they responded so readily to traditional methods of working between Glasgow and Carlisle. The new engines ran with the utmost freedom and steadiness downhill, and speeds of 85 m.p.h. and more were common. At the time these 4-6-0s were introduced there were no Pullman cars on the Anglo-Scottish trains; but since the inauguration of the through Midland service between St Pancras and Glasgow in 1876, the service to and from England was invariably referred to as the 'Pullmans'. The Manson 4-6-0s were economical engines on any count; but they were made even more so by the techniques of driving used by the men. At a later date two additional engines were built by Manson having superheaters, and these were probably the lightest engines on coal to be found anywhere in Great Britain at the time. All the Manson 4-6-0s passed into L.M.S.R. ownership; but by that time their day was practically over, and they were barely equal to the demands of the traffic.

NORTH BRITISH RAILWAY. 1906
A Reid 'Atlantic', a premier class engine.

In the early years of the twentieth century, as from its inception in 1876, the Midland and North British joint Anglo-Scottish service made heavy demands upon engine power between Edinburgh and Carlisle. In view of the gradients and the loads to be hauled a six-coupled engine would have seemed desirable; but because of the very bad curvature W. P. Reid decided upon an 'Atlantic', and he built the most powerful engine of the type ever to run in Great Britain. The first examples of the class were non-superheated, but after these had been modified their work became remarkable; both on the 'Waverley' route, and on the East Coast main line between Edinburgh and Aberdeen they took heavy loads, and climbed the steep gradients with a sureness and efficiency that helped to make the North British one of the most punctual railways in Great Britain. These massive engines, which all had fine Scottish names, looked their best in the original North British brown livery; but in London and North Eastern days they remained among the selected few pre-grouping types to be painted in the new standard apple-green, when most others were relegated to 'black'. In all they put in thirty years' work on the Aberdeen route, though they were displaced from the Waverley route a little earlier.

CALEDONIAN RAILWAYS. 1906

'Cardean', one of the most famous Scottish locomotives.

It is doubtful if any single locomotive built in the first decade of the twentieth century achieved, at the time, a fame greater than that enjoyed by the first of this small class of 5 locomotives. No. 903 was named *Cardean*, after the country estate of the Deputy Chairman of the Caledonian Board at that time, and in accordance with the practice of the day, so far as big engines on the Caledonian were concerned, it was allocated to one particular duty, and one only. *Cardean* had that veritable queen of Anglo-Scottish expresses, the 2 p.m. from Glasgow to Euston, which she took down to Carlisle. Then, after handing over to the L.&N.W.R., she brought the corresponding northbound express from Carlisle to Glasgow. And except for the very few occasions when she was under repair *Cardean* made that round trip every weekday for the best part of ten years! It was her unfailing reliability and excellent timekeeping that made the engine something of a legend – not only in Scotland but wherever there were railways. Technically *Cardean* and her four sister engines, none of which bore names, were a very large 4-6-0 development of the 'Dunalastairs', and their performance was enhanced in 1911–12 when they were fitted with superheaters. Simply and massively built, they were in every way an epitome of the neat, graceful British locomotives of the pre-1914 era.

LONDON, TILBURY AND SOUTHEND RAILWAY. 1907-9

Thomas Whitelegg's 4-4-2 express tank engine 'Thundersley'.

By the turn of the century residential traffic was rising to enormous proportions on the L.T.&S.R. line. The business trains were made up to the maximum length that could be accommodated in the platforms at Fenchurch Street station, and the most precise timekeeping prevailed. A late arrival of a Southend express had 'news value'. To keep abreast of traffic requirements Thomas Whitelegg reconstructed a batch of ten 4-4-2 tank engines originally put in service in 1897–8, giving them much larger boilers, new cylinders, and the very handsome appearance shown in our picture. These rebuilt engines did splendid work on the heavy business trains, and they were reinforced by four new engines to the same dimensions added to the stock in 1909. *Thundersley* was one of the 1909 batch, and was distinguished by having a polished casing to the safety valves. On all the other engines of the class this mounting was painted over green. The

Midland Railway absorbed the Tilbury line in 1912, and after the former company had become part of the L.M.S. system in 1923 twenty-five more were built in 1923–7, and a final ten as comparatively recently as 1930. This in itself is a great tribute to the efficiency of Thomas Whitelegg's design of 1907.

LONDON, BRIGHTON AND SOUTH COAST RAILWAY. 1910
The 'Abergavenny', Earle-Marsh's 4-6-2 tank engine for the Brighton line.

A natural sequel to the success of the 'I3' class of 4-4-2 tank engine, was the development of the design into something considerably larger to cope with the increasing loads of the fast trains between London and the South Coast towns. From the four-coupled 'I3' Marsh adopted the 4-6-2 wheel arrangement, a much longer and larger boiler, and larger cylinders. The latter needed to be of a size such that they could not be accommodated within the frames, but in the tradition of that period the outside cylinders, crossheads and connecting rods were arranged very neatly, and a very handsome engine resulted. Only two of these engines were built, for trial purposes, one in 1910 and the other in 1912, and they differed from each other in respect of the valve gear Engine No. 325 *Abergavenny*, as illustrated, had the Stephenson's link motion between the frames whereas No. 326 *Bessborough* had the Walschaerts radial valve gear, out-

side. Both did excellent work, and but for Marsh's retirement they would probably have become the standard express locomotives for the line. But Marsh's successor, L. B. Billinton, introduced still larger tank engines in later years. Although *Abergavenny* and *Bessborough* remained an isolated pair of engines they had a long life and did much valuable work. They were still on the steam-hauled Tunbridge Wells trains in 1947–8, and were not scrapped until 1951.

LONDON AND NORTH WESTERN RAILWAY. 1911

A 'Prince of Wales' 4-6-0, a very successful design.

These engines, like the 4-4-0 'George the Fifth' class, were a superheated development of a Whale design, and they proved the most generally useful passenger class the L.&N.W R ever possessed At the time of grouping the railways in 1922 the company had no fewer than 245 of them in service. In their early days they were classified for traffic purposes as the same as the 'George the Fifths', and indeed there was little to choose between the maximum efforts of the two classes. The 'Prince of Wales' was quite a small 4-6-0, though potentially the more powerful of the two classes in having a somewhat larger boiler and firebox. The 'Prince of Wales' became generally favoured on the heavy gradients between Lancaster and Carlisle, and by the time of grouping it was rare to see a 'George the Fifth' north of Preston. Engines of the 'Prince of Wales' class were engaged in trials against Midland, Caledonian, and Lancashire and Yorkshire engines

after the grouping. Although they did well so far as weight haulage was concerned the coal consumption was greater than that of the Midland compounds. The first 90 of the engines were named, in the old tradition of the L.&N.W.R., but with brass in short supply, naming was discontinued in the 155 engines built after the war. These engines were turned out in plain black, and the only adornment was the company's crest on the splashers.

LONDON AND SOUTH WESTERN RAILWAY. 1912
Dugald Drummond's handsome 'D15' 4-4-0 locomotive.

Following the conspicuous success of his 'T9' 'small' 4-4-0s Dugald Drummond built several classes of 4-4-0 for the L.&S.W.R. with larger boilers, and the class chosen for illustration is the 'D15', of which 10 were built in 1912. These very handsome engines included all the features of the 'T9' class, and as originally built they had the firebox water tubes. Like the 'T9s' they were very fast runners, but the enlarged boiler and proportions did not seem to give them as much extra capacity as was expected, and they did not really come into their own until Drummond's successor, R. W. Urie, fitted them with Eastleigh super-heaters, accompanied by an extended smokebox. Their very graceful appearance at the front end was somewhat impaired, but their performance was vastly improved. The 'D15' class was the last of a group of three large-boilered 4-4-0s of Drummond design, of which the others were the smaller-wheeled

'S11' class, designed for working on the hilly routes west of Exeter, and the 'L12', built in 1904-5. These latter were really a modified version of the 'T9', having the same chassis and machinery but with a larger boiler. In appearance they were very similar to the 'D15' class. Both the 'L12' and the 'D15' classes were long-lived; all the engines of both classes worked throughout the second World War, and passed into the ownership of the nationalized British Railways in 1948.

GREAT CENTRAL RAILWAY, 1913

J. G. Robinson's 'Director' class 4-4-0 express passenger engine.

The introduction of superheating led many locomotive engineers towards consideration of smaller engines to do the work previously entrusted to 'Atlantics' and 4-6-os, and the Great Central 'Director' class, of 1913, was an expression of this trend. These engines were designed to work through between London and Manchester, whereas the 'Atlantics' had usually to be changed at intermediate points. The first ten, built in 1913, were all named after directors of the company, though in the course of their long life two were re-named. Another 11 of a slightly enlarged design were built by the Great Central Railway in 1920, and it is one of these, No. 506 *Butler-Henderson* that has been preserved, and is housed in the Museum of Transport at Clapham. After grouping, another 24 of these fine engines were built specially for service in Scotland. Because of the reduced height of the loading gauge on the former North British Railway the Scottish engines had very much reduced chimneys and boiler mountings, and did not look so handsome in consequence. They all had names taken from characters in the Waverley novels, such as *Flora MacIvor*, *Haystoun of Bucklaw*, *Wizard of the Moor*, and *The Fiery Cross*. The original 'Directors' continued to do excellent work on the old Great Central line down to the year 1936, while the Scottish variants worked between Edinburgh, Dundee, Perth and Glasgow.

SOMERSET AND DORSET JOINT RAILWAY. 1914
One of the special 2-8-0 freight engines designed and built at Derby.

In meeting the responsibility for providing and maintaining locomotive power for this very difficult route the Midland Railway had to cope with grading conditions far worse than anything on their own line. A new type of 4-4-0 which with suitable adaptation subsequently became a Midland Railway standard, and later, in 1914, the Derby drawing office designed, for the S.D.J.R., a freight engine larger and more powerful than anything used on the Midland Railway proper. These very successful 2-8-0s, which came to put in nearly 50 years' service on the Somerset and Dorset line, were to some extent a synthesis of standard parts. They used the boiler of the standard superheated compound 4-4-0, though of course the use of outside cylinders and Walschaerts valve gear was new to Midland practice. To provide tractive power for hauling the freight trains on the 1 in 50 banks the cylinders were very large, 21 in. diameter by 28 in. stroke, and these could not easily have been accommodated inside. In their last years these engines, surprisingly enough, have done a considerable amount of passenger working, on summer Saturdays. Their high tractive power has enabled them to take heavier trains without assistance than the modern 4-6-0s, and this was invaluable at a time when there was a serious shortage of locomotives.

NORTH STAFFORDSHIRE RAILWAY. 1916

Hookham's 0-6-4 passenger tank engine.

The increasing weight of the Manchester–London expresses running via Stoke constituted something of a problem for the North Staffordshire locomotive department. Notwithstanding the fine work done by the Adams 4-4-2 tanks, a four-coupled engine was not ideal for such a steeply graded route, and in consequence J. A. Hookham designed a six-coupled engine with ample boiler capacity. It is interesting that he should have chosen the 0-6-4 type, because on some other railways engines of this wheel-arrangement had not been notably successful, or smooth in riding at express speed. The North Staffordshire engines on the Manchester–London expresses had not only to climb well, particularly on the heavy ascent that comes immediately after the restart at Macclesfield, but they had to run freely at speeds of over 60 m.p.h. The allowance for the 19·9 miles from Macclesfield to Stoke was only 27 min. The big 0-6-4 tanks did

their work well, and amply upheld the reputation of the North Staffordshire Railway. It is notable that its locomotive department at Stoke produced two engineers that came to render most distinguished service to the L.M.S.R. First there was T. Coleman, who became Chief Draughtsman to Sir William Stanier, and who worked out the design of the 'Coronation' Pacific of 1937, and then there was H. G. Ivatt, the last Chief Mechanical Engineer of the L.M.S.R.

SOUTH EASTERN AND CHATHAM RAILWAY. 1917
Maunsell's 'N' class 2-6-0 mixed traffic locomotive.

The retirement of Wainwright in 1913 led to a complete reorganization of the locomotive department of the S.E.&C.R. and although war conditions imposed serious restrictions upon all development work Maunsell and his staff did manage to produce, during the war, two new locomotives that proved the prototypes of much new construction afterwards. One of these was the 'N' class 2-6-0, a powerful general-utility design, which showed the influence of Great Western practice in the tapered boiler barrel, and the use of a long-lap, long-travel layout in the valve gear. In exterior design the pioneer 'N' class engine No. 810, had the plain, essentially functional look that characterized Maunsell's work in S.E.& C.R. days. Engine No. 810 was a great success in fast goods and intermediate passenger working, and multiplication of the design began soon after the end of the war. The 'N' class became a Southern Railway standard, and formed the basis

of a development of a family of similar engines, some with larger wheels, de-designed for light express traffic on heavily graded routes. The 'N' class had been used all over the Southern Railway system, and until 1945 it was responsible for the heaviest passenger workings west of Exeter.

MIDLAND RAILWAY. 1919
The Lickey Bank Engine 0-10-0 'Big Bertha'.

The Lickey Incline was always a formidable obstacle in the path of northbound trains on the West of England main line of the Midland Railway. The gradient is 1 in 37½ for 2 miles between Bromsgrove and Blackwell, and while 4-4-0 engines of the No. 2 Class would bring loads of 250 tons or even more up from Bristol, substantial assistance in rear was always needed up the Lickey Incline. A number of 0-6-0 tank engines were kept in steam at Bromsgrove to assist every north-bound train, and with the heavier trains two and sometimes even three bank engines were necessary. The 10-coupled tender engine, nicknamed 'Big Bertha', was designed to do the work of two 0-6-0 engines. She was by far the largest and heaviest locomotive ever built by the Midland Railway, and fully justified the claims made for her. It certainly needed careful management of the fire before an ascent to keep those four large cylinders adequately supplied with steam during the 7 or 8 minutes of heavy pounding up the incline. But from her construction in 1919, she did the job for 30 years. She must have been unique among main line engines in having so limited a sphere of activity. All her work throughout those 30 years was done between Bromsgrove South and Blackwell – a distance of less than 3 miles. The only times when she went further afield were her periodic visits to Derby Works for overhaul.

23

FURNESS RAILWAY. 1920

E. Sharples's 4-6-4 tank engine for heavy intermediate duty.

Apart from the mail trains, and the connections to London and North Western long-distance expresses at Carnforth, most of the passenger working on the Furness Railway consisted of smartly-timed stopping trains. Before the large-scale introduction of private motoring there was a surprising amount of station-to-station passenger business. Various types of locomotives were used ranging from Pettigrew's latest 4-4-0s, to 0-6-2 tank engines, and after World War I the need was felt for larger engines. On short runs a tank engine has a considerable advantage, and E. Sharples prepared designs for the neat and powerful 4-6-4 that is illustrated. Much larger than anything that had preceded them on the Furness Railway these engines made short work of all kinds of traffic. They accelerated from rest with great rapidity, and ran freely at speeds of 50 to 55 m.p.h. They were well liked for their smooth riding and easy action, but their life in

the Furness Railway livery was short. After grouping they were painted in Midland red, and as such looked very handsome; but after a short time 'red' was reserved only for the top-link express locomotives, and all other classes were painted in black. But whether in 'iron-ore' red, 'Midland red', or black, the 'Big Jumbos', as they were known, filled a very useful niche in Furness Railway operating.

METROPOLITAN RAILWAY. 1920
Charles Jones's 4-4-4 express tank engine.

Beginning with the purely Underground section from Bishops Road to Farringdon Street, opened in 1863, the Metropolitan Railway extended far out beyond the northern suburbs of London, to Aylesbury, and Verney Junction through a delightful part of the Chiltern Hills, in Buckinghamshire. Claiming it for themselves the railway exhorted town-dwellers to live in 'Metroland', and a number of very attractive services were run from Verney Junction, Aylesbury, and Chesham to the City. Luxurious bogie coaches were introduced and some trains even had a Pullman car. They were electrically hauled as far as Harrow-on-the-Hill, and then there was a change-over to steam. Some smart running was required on these popular residential trains, and after a trial of 0-6-4 tank engines, Jones introduced the handsome and efficient 4-4-4 tanks shown in our picture. These engines had to run fast, but were also required to climb well, because the line

north of Rickmansworth mounts into the Chiltern Hills on a continuous gradient of 1 in 100. Though there was much express running on the London side of Rickmansworth, beyond that point the Metropolitan trains called at all stations, and hard work was involved in getting away from Chorley Wood, and Chalfont Road, against the continuous rising gradient. These engines did the job most competently.

GREAT NORTHERN RAILWAY. 1922

The first Gresley Pacific, No. 1470 'Great Northern'.

The building of the two prototype 'Pacific' engines Nos. 1470 and 1471 at Doncaster Works in 1922 marked the beginning of a new locomotive era in Great Britain. Although an experimental Pacific had been built by the Great Western Railway as long previously as 1908 that engine, No. 111 *The Great Bear*, had been an isolated unit, and formed no part of the standard pattern of locomotive operating on the G.W.R. On the other hand the Great Northern 'Pacifics' were destined to become an L.N.E.R. standard for all important express train working between London and Edinburgh, and with their success and ever increasing prowess the term 'big engine' took on a new meaning in the nineteen-twenties. But to revert to their first introduction, in size and tractive power they represented just as great an advance over the Ivatt 'Atlantics' as the latter engines did over the Stirling eight-foot 'singles'. Yet revolu-

tionary though they were in size they represented an entirely logical step in the development, and their design was entirely in the Doncaster tradition. In the case of so great an advance in size it could hardly be expected that finality in design would be achieved at once. After some years alterations to the valve gear were found desirable. But from 1927, after these changes had been made, the design, in its performance no less than its bold conception, became one of the classics of British steam locomotive history.

NORTH EASTERN RAILWAY. 1922

Sir Vincent Raven's Pacific, the climax of North Eastern locomotive design.

The North Eastern Railway had a very long tradition of excellent and individualistic locomotive design, and just before the railway itself became merged into the L.N.E.R. group, the last Chief Mechanical Engineer, Sir Vincent Raven, produced the first of his huge Pacifics. These engines, of which five were built at Darlington Works, were a natural development from the very successful three-cylinder Atlantics of Class 'Z'. In this respect they were unlike the contemporary 'Pacifics' of Sir Nigel Gresley, on the Great Northern. The latter represented an entirely new concept in design from Doncaster works rather than a straight enlargement of the previous 'Atlantic' engines. The Raven Pacifics were a pure enlargement in boiler and length, and in the perpetuation of the use of three sets of Stephenson link motion for actuating the valves. When Gresley was appointed Chief Mechanical Engineer of the L.N.E.R. he had to decide which 'Pacific' design to adopt as a future standard. Other things being equal he would naturally be inclined to favour his own design; but in trials with the dynamometer car between Doncaster and Kings Cross in 1923 the Great Northern engine showed a definite superiority over her North Eastern rival. Nevertheless the N.E.R. did some excellent work, and as the final expression of North Eastern design practice these Raven 'Pacifics' occupy a notable place in locomotive history.

LONDON AND NORTH EASTERN RAILWAY. 1935
Gresley's class A4 streamlined Pacific 'Mallard' which attained 126 m.p.h. in 1938.

These world-famous engines represented the consummation of Pacific locomotive development at Doncaster. Into them Gresley put those finishing touches to the already very successful 'A3', in the form of still higher boiler pressure, larger diameter piston valves, and the internal streamlining of steam ports and passages. These features substantially improved the haulage capacity and speed of the engines, while the form of the external streamlining fairly captured popular imagination. The first four engines were designed for the Silver Jubilee high speed service, and when the pioneer engine, No. 2509 *Silver Link* attained a maximum speed of 112 m.p.h. on its very first public trip the fame of the class was assured. From this spectacular beginning the 'A4s' went from strength to strength. They hauled tremendous loads at express speeds; they frequently topped 100 m.p.h. in ordinary service, and in 1938 *Mallard* made the world record for

steam traction with a speed of 126 m.p.h. After the first four 'silver' engines, garter blue became the standard colour for the class, in L.N.E.R. days. They remained in first class express service until 1962, one of the finest of their latter-day achievements being the haulage each summer of the Elizabethan express, non-stop over the 392¾ miles between Kings Cross and Edinburgh, in 6½ hours an average speed of 60½ m.p.h. with load of about 420 tons.

SOUTHERN RAILWAY. 1941
'Merchant Navy' class Pacific designed by O.V.S. Bulleid.

The appointment of Mr O. V. S. Bulleid as Chief Mechanical Engineer of the Southern Railway, was the signal for a strong revival in steam locomotive activity. For some years previously nearly all attention had been concentrated on the extension of the electrified system. In the new 'Pacific' design of 1941 many features were included to combat the gradually worsening conditions of railway operation. The boiler and firebox were designed to use low-grade fuel; extensive use of welding was made in the construction of both boiler and chassis, to reduce weight; and to minimize maintenance work on the running gear the valve gear was totally enclosed in an oil bath. The exterior casing was of striking form, and the final touch of novelty was provided by the Box-poc form of driving wheels. Our picture shows one of these engines as originally built, in the pre-war Southern livery of malachite green. Additional cowling had to be introduced at a later date for smoke deflection at the front end. These engines proved very fast and powerful, but unfortunately some of the innovations, and particularly the valve gear, were troublesome and expensive to maintain. In later years the air-smoothed casings were removed, and a conventional Walschaerts valve gear fitted in place of the totally enclosed gear of special design.

29

LONDON, MIDLAND AND SCOTTISH RAILWAY. 1943

The rebuilt 'Royal Scot' which included many new features and the Stanier taper boiler.

The original 'Royal Scots' were very good engines for their day. But they included the conventional design of parallel boiler, and straight-sided Belpaire firebox. When the time came for replacement of the original boilers a decision was taken to fit new boilers, having the tapered barrel and other features of detail design that had proved so free from trouble, and so efficient in steam raising on the smaller 4-6-os of the L.M.S.R. At the same time a more extensive rebuild of the entire engine was undertaken, providing new cylinders and valves, with the same advanced features of design that had proved so successful on the 'Coronation' Pacifics of 1937. The changes made a considerable difference in the outward appearance of the engines, but they made a remarkable improvement in the performance, so much so that in 1948, when the nationalized British Railways conducted a series of test runs between locomotives of the former privately-owned companies, the 'Rebuilt Royal Scots' were able to compete on very nearly equal terms with 'Pacifics' from other railways, although the difference in weight between these 4-6-os and their competitors ranged from between 10 to 20 tons. Eventually all 70 engines of the 'Royal Scot' class were rebuilt in conformity with this most successful modernization.

BRITISH RAILWAYS. 1951
A 'Britannia' Pacific No. 70037 'Hereward the Wake'.

As a result of the Interchange trials of 1948 the engineers of the Railway Executive of the British Transport Commission, under the direction of Mr R. A. Riddles, the member for mechanical and electrical engineering, designed a series of new standard locomotives embodying features shown to be most satisfactory in the performance of the former companies' locomotives. The first of these new designs to appear was the Class 7MT 'Pacific'. To emphasize its national rather than regional character the first of these engines was named *Britannia*, while others have been named after famous locomotives of the past, and famous characters in British history, literature, and fiction. The engine illustrated, No. 70037 *Hereward the Wake*, was in regular service in East Anglia. The 'Britannia's' might, in other circumstances, have had as long and distinguished a career as many of their predecessors in British locomotive history. But the decision to supersede steam traction entirely was made in 1955, and replacement of the 'Britannia's' by diesel-electric locomotives began in 1958. During their short career on express work, in East Anglia, on the Western Region, on the Irish Mails, and on the Continental expresses of the Southern the 'Britannia's' did much excellent work, with economic use of fuel.

INDEX

G715/7.5M/10/77(W